MACHU PICCHU:

Mystery City of the Incas

❖❖❖❖❖❖❖❖

by
Lorraine F. McConnell

cpi
contemporary perspectives, inc.

This book is distributed by Silver Burdett Company, Morristown, New Jersey 07960.

Library of Congress Number: 78-22058

Art and Photo Credits

Cover photo, Laurie Nadel
Illustrations on pages 5, 14, 16, 29, 31, 37, and 44, by Steve Oliva, Mere Images, Inc.
Reprinted courtesy of Coronet Instructional Media, a division of Esquire, Inc.
Illustration on page 7, Culver Pictures
Photo on page 9, Dave Maenza/F.P.G.
Photos on pages 13, 17, 19, 21, 23, 25, 42, 45, and 47, Laurie Nadel
Photo on page 27, Dick Swift/F.P.G.
Photo on page 35, Hallinan/Alpha
Photo on page 39, Tom Grill/F.P.G.
Photo on page 41, Maurice and Sally Landre/F.P.G.
Every effort has been made to trace the ownership of all copyrighted material in this
book and obtain permission for its use.

Library of Congress Cataloging in Publication Data

McConnell, Lorraine F. 1949-
    Machu picchu: mystery city of the Incas

    SUMMARY: Describes the discovery in 1911 of the Peruvian ruins called Machu
Picchu and presents the various theories of the function of this city in the ancient
Inca civilization.
    1. Machu Picchu, Peru—Juvenile literature. 2. Incas—Juvenile literature. [1.
Machu Picchu, Peru. 2. Incas] I. Title.
F3429.1.M3M37   985'.3   78-22058
ISBN 0-89547-069-1

Manufactured in the United States of America
ISBN 0-89547-069-1

Contents

❖ Chapter 1 ❖

Search for the Lost City

❖❖❖❖❖❖❖❖❖❖❖❖❖

The young teacher and his group made camp on a sandy beach beside a river. They had been walking and climbing for two weeks. Now they were so tired that some wondered if they could go on. How could they ever get their leader to turn back? He was a teacher, and teachers want to know the truth. To him, this search was the most important thing in the world.

They had crossed snow-capped mountains. Slowly they had made their way down steep rock walls. They had cut their way through dense forests where the rain never stopped. And the land ahead of them would be even harder to get through. Even the guides wanted to turn back. The men sat listening to the sound of the river beside them. No one said a word; each was lost in his own thoughts. Finally, one of them broke the silence. His words were a warning.

"These mountains are filled with hungry cougars and deadly snakes."

The others looked up at the sound of his voice.
Now that the silence was broken, more voices were
heard.

"There are Indians around here ... the most savage
Indians you'll find anywhere. If one of their poisoned
arrows even nicks you, you're a goner!"

Still the teacher sat quietly. He too was frightened. The very roar of the river seemed to warn him of dangers that lay ahead. The climbing would be extremely dangerous. They would have to watch out for wild animals — and worse, for wild men. The teacher knew all these things. But he knew one thing more. He would never give up.

He answered the others in the only way he could. "We will climb again in the morning."

Who were these men? Where were they? Why did their leader tell the others that they had to finish what they had begun? Who was this leader?

His name was Hiram Bingham, and he was a teacher of South American history at Yale University. The National Geographic Society had helped him and his group start on their long journey into a mysterious land. Bingham's team was made up of a naturalist (an expert on nature), a surgeon, a topographer (an expert to make maps of the area), and an engineer. The rest of the small group were South American natives. They were to guide the men through a little-known part of the world.

The expedition was traveling in the part of South America where the Andes Mountains rise high above the Urubamba River in Peru. Many people had visited

Hiram Bingham, Yale professor and discoverer of Machu Picchu, was also a U.S. senator from Connecticut (1925-1933).

this land before. But very few had come back to tell about it.

Professor Bingham himself had been to other parts of these mountains. But now, in July 1911, he had a reason to return. He had found some ruins in the mountains. They were the ruins of palaces, temples, and houses. No one had lived there since the days of the great Inca Empire in the sixteenth century. But Bingham believed there were still other ruins — more important ones too — much higher up in the Central Andes.

The Andes Mountains are the second-highest mountain range on earth. It is almost impossible to climb their tallest peaks. And Bingham had only a few clues to help him find the ruins he was looking for. Yet that did not matter. Bingham knew he *had* to explore that part of the mountains known as Inca Land.

Whenever anyone asked him why he wanted to climb such dangerous mountains, he answered simply. "Above all, I want to find the last capital of the Incas."

Now Bingham was in the Urubamba Valley. He was so very close to those mountain peaks he wanted to see. He had no thought of turning back.

In the beginning, Bingham's team had been anxious to climb two mountains more than any others. One was called Huayna Picchu. It means Young Man Peak. The other, Machu Picchu, means Old Man Peak. But by now the men were all tired to the bone. It seemed as if no one wanted to go on climbing. It seemed as if no one *could* climb. Bingham heard only words of argument.

The peaks of the Andes Mountains rise high above the jungles of Peru.

"Is there really such a place as this capital of the Incas?" someone asked.

"Nothing has ever been written about a city in those mountains," another said. "Surely the Spaniards would have found it when they conquered the Incas."

Bingham knew all this. He also knew that no such city could be found on Raimondi's map. Antonio Raimondi was a great explorer of the mid-1800s. He spent his life exploring Peru. He made a map of the Urubamba Valley and the mountains around it. According to him, there were no cities on Machu Picchu or Huayna Picchu.

But Professor Bingham was fascinated by those mountain peaks. They stood nearly two miles above sea level. He couldn't stop thinking of the famous words of Rudyard Kipling.

"Go and look behind the ranges — something lost behind the ranges. Lost and waiting for you. Go!"

❖ Chapter 2 ❖
The Discovery
❖❖❖❖❖❖❖❖❖❖❖❖❖❖❖

The morning of July 24 dawned in a cold drizzle.
The men looked at the river that flowed down from the
mountaintop. No one wanted to climb the gorge that
led up the steep slope.

The naturalist gave an excuse to stay put. "There are
more butterflies down here near the river," he said.
He was sure he could discover some new kind.

The surgeon said he had to wash and sew his
clothes. The others also found reasons for not making
the dangerous climb. So Bingham set out with just two
of the guides. He had to pay them extra money.

The climb would have been very hard even for
skilled mountaineers. And it was made worse by the
great heat. Even though in July it is winter in Peru,
the sun burned down on the men. The higher they
climbed, the hotter it got. They spent hours chopping
with knives through tangled forest growth. They had
to make their way over boulders as big as four-story
houses. They found themselves crawling along
slippery rock slopes. There was nothing on these
slopes to keep them from falling straight down —
thousands of feet into the valley below.

Even so, they kept on climbing. Up ... up ... slowly up the mountain ....

They came to a rocky bank of the river. They had to cross it. There was only a bridge made of thin logs tied together with vines. Anyone who fell from that bridge would be dashed to pieces on the river's jagged rocks.

Now even Bingham thought they would have to turn back. It was hard to hear above the noise of the roaring river, but the guides thought they heard Bingham say: "No one could live for a second in those rapids."

Bingham was not thinking of himself. He did not want to risk the lives of his guides. Did this mean that he was going to give up the search that had taken so long?

At that moment something happened that made Bingham's eyes open wide with surprise. He saw the two guides take off their shoes. Now, they went slowly across the bridge. They gripped the logs with their toes.

The guides were willing to continue the dangerous trip! They did not even wait to be told! Bingham

Bingham's group climbed treacherous mountain slopes high above the Urubamba River. ▶

followed quickly. He started to crawl across the bridge.

He was halfway to the opposite bank when the wind suddenly came up. The bridge began swinging wildly. Bingham lost his grip on the log. It was the end!

Somehow he was able to grab one of the vines. Slowly he pulled himself back up on the log. And then, finally, he was on the other side of the river.

The three men began climbing once more. They climbed for hours. The air became damp. It was getting hard to breathe. The air is very thin on the upper slopes of high mountains. Bingham and the guides were so tired they could hardly stand.

And still they kept climbing. At last, they reached the top of the gorge!

But had the terrible climb been worth all the trouble? Bingham looked around him. He could see no sign of an old city anywhere. He almost wanted to cry with disappointment.

Suddenly two Indians appeared. Who were they? Who could possibly live so far from other people? Were these the people with the deadly poisoned arrows?

Bingham and his guides were in for a surprise. The Indians smiled and held out their hands. "Welcome," they said. Then they gave the strangers fresh water and sweet potatoes.

Imagine the professor's astonishment! Here, 9,000 feet above sea level, he had found two Indians living in a grass hut with their wives and families.

Bingham and the guides spent some time refreshing themselves after the climb. The Indians were named Richarte and Alvarez. They told how they had come to this spot far from other people. It seemed they just wanted to farm and make their home.

"No officials looking for army volunteers," said Alvarez. "Or collecting taxes," Richarte admitted.

The men talked a while longer. Later, the professor left the cool shade of the hut to look around. He was guided by one of the Indian's sons. They walked along

16

a ridge. Soon they reached a steep hill. There were steps carved into it. The little boy quickly walked up. He called back to Bingham: "Climb."

Bingham did as he was told, never expecting the marvel that was waiting for him. With the boy, he walked just a few feet further.

And suddenly, through the trees that grew everywhere, he saw the ruins!

Bingham was amazed to find the ruins of an ancient city so high in the mountains.

Everything was partly hidden by trees and vines that had been growing for centuries. Still, the shapes became clearer and clearer as Bingham pushed his way through the thick bushes. Walls of ruined houses sprang up before him. Everywhere! A temple . . . an altar . . . monuments! A treasure of buildings spread in every direction around him.

The little boy could see that Bingham was amazed. But he had no idea why. He just knew that parts of this place were good for growing vegetables. Other parts were good for playing.

Professor Bingham was walking about quickly. He was more amazed with every step. Here was an entire city! It had been built high in the sky on a saddle between two magnificent mountains. Here, overlooking the Grand Canyon of the Urubamba River, he had discovered an Inca city that had been lost for ages. What city was it? Questions ran through his head: Why was this city built? Who had lived in it? When was it built? Why was it abandoned?

The ancient city lay hidden between mountain peaks, untouched for centuries until Bingham found it. ▶

✿ Chapter 3 ✿
International Fame
✿✿✿✿✿✿✿✿✿✿✿✿✿✿✿

Through stories in the *National Geographic* magazine, the world soon learned of the lost city of Machu Picchu. (Bingham didn't know the name of the city. So he named it after the mountain that was beside it.) The professor was treated like a hero in the United States.

But soon he returned to Peru to explore the city he had found. He wanted to learn as much as he could about it. So did many others.

In fact, Bingham's discovery started a great argument among archeologists — people who study ancient peoples. Even today, these scholars can't agree. The big questions still haven't been answered. Who lived in the Inca city now known as Machu Picchu? And why?

Even with many workmen helping, it took Bingham four months to clear the jungle-smothered city. But what he finally uncovered astonished the entire world!

Machu Picchu was a city three square miles in size. The amazing thing was that it had hardly changed. It is today just as it was 400 years ago when the Incas lived

A memorial to Hiram Bingham reads: Homage to Hiram Bingham on the 50th anniversary of the discovery of Machu Picchu: 1911 — July 24 — 1961.

there. All of the other Inca cities were destroyed by the Spanish conquistadors. The Spaniards tore down the buildings in the cities they conquered because of the gold and silver in them.

But because Machu Picchu was so difficult to get to, the Spaniards never found it. And it had remained untouched until Bingham found it.

More than 200 different buildings were found in the old city. Most of them were built with the very best Inca stonework. There were many temples. One had a big wall shaped like a half circle — a very hard thing to build! There were also an altar, a huge sundial, many houses, and row after row of terraces that were cut in the hillside for growing crops. A system of stairways connected the different parts of the city. They were all carved by hand.

The stones that made up the buildings were bigger than a man. Some weighed 10 or 15 tons. They had all been polished until they were as smooth as glass!

How did the Incas lift these huge stones and put them in place? They had no machines or horses or other strong animals. It is possible that hundreds of men worked together using nothing but long tree-trunk levers to lift the stones. Most experts agree with that idea.

The stonework of Machu Picchu ▶ was all done without machines.

It is also clear that there must have been hundreds of fine craftsmen working to shape the stones and give them a smooth finish. The Incas had no iron tools, but they fitted the stones together so perfectly that cement wasn't even needed. Some of the stones are so close that not even a razor blade can be slipped between them! It isn't surprising that these temples and houses have stood for centuries!

Professor Bingham saw other buildings that were made later, by people using better tools and equipment. The newer buildings had fallen because of earthquakes or old age. Yet the Incas had built walls that were not only beautiful but amazingly strong!

Bingham and other experts still didn't know why Machu Picchu had been built, who had lived there, or why the city had been deserted. But they thought they were beginning to find some answers. The Incas had put up this great city only 60 miles away from their capital city, Cuzco. They must have had a good reason.

If the archeologists looked long enough, could they find the real reason? There were *some* clues.

The buildings of Machu Picchu have lasted for centuries. And they were built without cement! ▶

❁ Chapter 4 ❁
Clues and Legends
❁❁❁❁❁❁❁❁❁❁❁❁

Since Professor Bingham found Machu Picchu, many other experts have tried to piece together the clues. But no one has really yet learned the history of this ancient city.

If the Incas had a written language, there would be less mystery. But their language, called Quichua, was only spoken. Almost everything we know about the Incas has been passed down in legends. If anything was written about them, it was written by the Spaniards. And the Spaniards didn't always tell the truth about the people they conquered.

Luckily, Machu Picchu itself gives many hints about those who lived there many centuries ago.

One of the most important parts of Machu Picchu is the Sacred Plaza. It is here that a beautiful semicircular temple stands. Nearby are the temples to the Sun, Moon, and the Stars. Close to these temples Professor Bingham found the great sundial. It was called the Intihuatana. In the Quichua language, this means "the place to which the sun is tied."

The little Indian farm boy might have used this large sundial as a playground. But the Incas had another

The sundial found at Machu Picchu stands in the Sacred Plaza.

purpose for it. Here the Inca priests prayed to the Sun, which was the God of their religion. They also tried to tie the Sun God to the Intihuatana. If they could do that, they believed, the weather would be warmer and they would have better crops.

The Intihuatana at Machu Picchu was the largest sundial that had been found in Peru. And there were so many beautiful temples. Could this mean that *the whole city* of Machu Picchu was built as a place of religious worship?

27

Professor Bingham thought so. But he needed more proof. He thought he might have it if he could find the burial grounds. The remains of the people buried in Machu Picchu would give important clues. They would tell Bingham about the kind of life led centuries ago. So far, Bingham had found no skeletons. Then he had an idea. He thought it would make the workers hunt harder.

"A Peruvian silver dollar to anyone who finds a cave with a skull inside," he offered.

The idea seemed to work. The men hunted around the dangerous cliffs. They cut through the vines and jungle weeds. Many bled from deep scratches. Their clothes were torn almost to ribbons. They searched all through the city. Still they found nothing.

And Bingham began to ask himself: "Could it be possible there were no graves at all?"

But finally Richarte and Alvarez, the Indian farmers, found the first burial caves. They had planted their crops all around the city. So they knew the place better than anyone else. They led the professor to a ledge. It was under a ridge that was covered with moss.

Sure enough. "The bones of a woman!" Bingham exclaimed.

Machu Picchu may have been a convent for "chosen" women.

Richarte and Alvarez led them to seven more hidden caves. All of them contained the bones of women only. Where were the bones of the men who had lived in Machu Picchu?

The workers continued looking. Finally they had found all of the bones in the caves and cemeteries. Everyone was surprised at what they discovered. Of 173 skeletons, 150 were those of women!

Professor Bingham thought he knew the reason. "This must have been like a convent," he said excitedly. "Its inhabitants were the Chosen Women of the Sun!"

But many people wanted to know more. What did "the Chosen Women of the Sun" mean? Who were these women? And how was this proof that Machu Picchu was a place of religious worship?

Professor Bingham explained that the Inca rulers and nobles had many wives and handmaidens to serve them. The prettiest young girls were sent to live in schools in certain sacred cities. There they learned to weave beautiful garments. They were taught to prepare special foods and drinks. They worshiped the Sun God and the Inca nobles who claimed to speak for the Sun God.

Professor Bingham believed that Machu Picchu was one of these sacred cities. The Chosen Women learned to worship the Sun God there and to be handmaidens to the noble Incas.

He thought about the women's skeletons that had been found. The few skeletons of men were not those of strong warriors. They were the bones of smaller, weaker men. The only men allowed in the sacred cities were priests, so the male skeletons at Machu Picchu must have been priests. All of the others were Chosen Women. They were never allowed to leave. And except for the priests, no men were allowed to enter.

There is a folk story about one of these Chosen Women who did try to leave the city. Her name was

Legend says that a woman and her lover who tried to escape from Machu Picchu were turned to stone.

Chuqui Llantu. It means "Fleeting Shadow." One day Chuqui Llantu was walking in the fields near the city. Accidentally she met a man. He was not a noble Inca. In fact, he was only a llama herdsman. Chuqui should not even have talked to him. But she fell in love with the young man.

The city was guarded at all of the gates. Even so, Chuqui was able to escape somehow. She ran into the arms of the young herdsman. The legend says that the gods were angry with the young couple for being disloyal. The gods changed poor Chuqui Llantu and the herdsman into stone.

Professor Bingham thought about what he had learned:

• There were many temples and places of worship at Machu Picchu. These were dedicated to the Sun God.

• The stonework on the buildings was very beautiful. These buildings must have been made for the Inca rulers.

• Most of the people who had lived in Machu Picchu were women. These must have been the Chosen Women.

Then, after more study, Bingham made a startling announcement about the place he called Machu Picchu. He said: "This was the site of ancient Vilcapampa."

According to the writings of the Spaniards, there was definitely a place called Vilcapampa, though they were never allowed to see this place. They were told that it was a sacred city. The Inca rulers lived there. Also, a University of Idolatry was located there. This means a school where idol worship and prayer were studied.

But was this enough proof? Could Professor Bingham say that Machu Picchu was really the ancient city of Vilcapampa?

Archeologists and other experts disagreed. They had their own ideas about this city of mystery.

Chapter 5

A Royal Hotel or a Royal Hiding Place?

❖❖❖❖❖❖❖❖❖❖❖❖❖❖

A historian named Burr C. Brundage thinks that Machu Picchu was a place where the Inca rulers went to relax.

Brundage says the city was built by a great Inca leader named Pachacuti. He ruled in about 1450. Pachacuti was one of the first Inca emperors to get more land for his people. He did this by conquering many nearby countries. Among the people the Incas defeated were the Collas. The Incas were never known to be kind to those they defeated.

It is possible that Pachacuti wanted a vacation spot for himself. Machu Picchu, as we know, was built of huge boulders. Pachacuti might have forced large groups of Collas to carve a special road up the mountain. Then the Collas could have been made to carry those heavy rocks up to the place where Pachacuti wanted his city built.

If this idea is correct, Pachacuti could not have picked a more beautiful spot. High in the mountains,

Machu Picchu's magnificent setting was a fitting place for a hero to spend his last years.

The Inca leaders ruled their country from the military headquarters at Vitcos. From time to time they surely needed a place where they could relax. Might they have gone to Pachacuti's city high on Machu Picchu? No one is certain.

But the idea is far from impossible.

Another theory is that Machu Picchu was used as a place to hide from the Spaniards.

Philip II, the king of Spain, sent the conquistadors to invade Peru in 1533. Their leader, Francisco Pizarro, had heard that the Incas used gold in building their temples. This was true. The Incas believed that gold was the tears wept by the Sun God. They kept the gold in the temples dedicated to him.

At that time, King Philip was deeply in debt and needed the gold. So the Spaniards were sent to loot the Inca cities and conquer the people. The two peoples waged war. The Incas fought hard, but their spears were no match for the Spaniards' guns. With ease, the conquistadors took Cuzco, the Incas' capital city. Then they went on to destroy all of the local towns.

The Inca leaders escaped with their families and some trusted warriors. They went into the jungles and

When the Spaniards invaded Peru in the 1500s, the Inca leaders may have escaped to mountaintop cities like Machu Picchu.

the mountains beyond. The journey was so difficult that the Spaniards could not follow. They tried many times. But the roaring Urubamba River stopped them. The soldiers could find no way to cross.

Did the Inca rulers who got away from the Spaniards hide up in the mountains? Were they living safely in the city now known as Machu Picchu?

It seems possible. Machu Picchu might have been built as a fort. It was built on a site that is naturally protected on all sides. The peaks of Huayna Picchu and Machu Picchu rise high around the city. And on three sides of the town a steep gorge drops straight down into the Urubamba River.

Two other pieces of evidence point strongly to the idea that Machu Picchu was a fortress. These are the two signal stations built on top of Huayna Picchu and Machu Picchu mountains. From both stations, guards were in control of the valley below. They could sight the enemy far in the distance. Word could be sent to the city right away. As the enemy soldiers climbed the steep mountain, they could be killed by boulders rolled down from the heights.

Those signal stations must have been very important to the Incas. Each was at the very edge of a high peak. If any of the workmen slipped while lifting the rocks in place, they would have fallen 3,000 feet — more than half a mile.

Some experts feel that the signal stations would not have been built unless Machu Picchu was a military stronghold. There, the last noble Incas could live

Surrounded by high peaks, the city was safe from enemies.

protected from the Spaniards. They surely would have been captured if they left the city.

There is yet another theory about Machu Picchu. Some think the Incas might have built the place to try out a new kind of farming.

When Bingham was greeted by the Indian farmers, Richarte and Alvarez, he noticed that they grew their crops on stone-walled terraces. This could be evidence that Machu Picchu was really used for agriculture.

Living high in the mountains where few plants can grow, the Incas had to build terraces and fill them with soil. First they carried good soil up from the river banks. Then they held the soil in place with rows of large rocks. These rocks held in the moisture, helping to keep the soil fertile. The stone terraces helped the Incas raise crops in places where there had been no soil.

Was Machu Picchu built to grow the best crops of all — and the biggest? Were the Incas looking for a better way to grow richer crops of maize and potatoes?

Many Inca cities had terraces to grow crops. But the terracing at Machu Picchu was large enough to grow more food for more people than could ever have lived there. The stone-faced terraces seem to go on forever. Each is hundreds of feet long and ten feet high. And each was built so well that Richarte and Alvarez were using the same soil 400 years later!

What were the Incas doing with all those terraces? Perhaps Machu Picchu fed the entire Inca nation!

But if that is so, how can we explain the great temples and altars? What were the signal stations?

The Incas farmed on terraces, which kept the soil from slipping down the steep mountain slopes.

Was Machu Picchu really a farm *and* a place of worship *and* a vacation spot *and* a fortress? Or was it none of these at all?

Machu Picchu could have been many things — a farm, a convent, a fortress, or a hideaway.

There may be a way to choose the best of those possibilities. The legend of the Temple of the Three Windows just might be the key.

❖ Chapter 6 ❖

The Temple of the Three Windows

❖❖❖❖❖❖❖❖❖❖❖❖❖❖❖

The Incas, like all people, had many myths and legends. The legend of the Temple of the Three Windows is one of the most famous.

Manco Capac was the first ruler to be called an Inca, the king of the people. Manco Capac was born in a cave some time in the late twelfth century, near the small village of Tampu-tocco. When Manco grew up, he set out with his two brothers to win new lands for his people. He conquered many places and made good laws. Manco began the line of Inca kings that eventually conquered most of Peru, Ecuador, and Bolivia as well as parts of Chile and Argentina.

Manco became known as a powerful chief and a lucky warrior. People came from far away to bring him rich gifts. Thankful for his good fortune, he ordered a monument to be set up in Tampu-tocco — his birthplace. He wanted a temple built there which was to have three windows on one wall. The windows were

Manco's people brought gifts of gold to the powerful ruler.

dedicated to Manco's ancestors. They were to look out onto a canyon. To Manco, they stood for the caves that he and his brothers came from. The story says that the three brothers went forth from the caves of their birth to take over the land before them.

No such building was ever seen — until 1911, when Bingham reached Machu Picchu. He discovered a monument exactly like the one Manco had ordered! It was a temple with three windows that faced out over the canyon toward the rising sun. The designs of the wall and the windows were unlike anything else in all of Peru!

Bingham was already convinced that Machu Picchu had been called Vilcapampa at one time. But now he believed that at an earlier time it was known by another name. He was convinced that the name of the older part of Machu Picchu was Tampu-tocco.

Was this the main clue to the history of Machu Picchu? Was Machu Picchu really the birthplace of the first Inca, Manco Capac?

The Temple of Three Windows is an example of the masterful temples the Incas built.

Archeologists say that different parts of Machu Picchu were built at different times. So, perhaps Machu Picchu also had different *names* at different times. And its *first* name could have been Tampu-tocco!

But no one has yet been able to prove this.

In the meanwhile, one of Professor Bingham's other ideas has been proved wrong — the belief that Machu Picchu had once been called Vilcapampa. Many people had agreed with this — until 1966, when a man parachuted into the Andes Mountains not far from Machu Picchu. There he came across the ruins of an ancient city. It had been burned and almost completely destroyed by the Spaniards. But just enough was found in the rubble to show that this city had in fact been the real Vilcapampa.

Would other ideas be proved wrong? Would Machu Picchu's mystery keep growing?

Many people visit Machu Picchu today. It is a popular tourist attraction. The path up the mountain is much easier to climb than it was when Bingham risked his life in 1911 to reach the city. You can take a bus right up the steep road that leads directly to Machu Picchu itself. You can even stay in a small hotel outside the entrance to the city. Except for that hotel, Machu Picchu is exactly the same as it was in the golden age of the Incas.

46

People from all over the world climb the ancient stairways to explore Machu Picchu. They marvel at the clever farming system. They are awed as they gaze at the architectural designs — all done by a civilization without power plants, without factories, without even a written language!

Everyone who visits Machu Picchu still wonders about the city that seemed to vanish from the earth for hundreds of years.

The experts have given us many ideas about this magnificent place. But we can be sure of only one thing — it has been a mystery ever since it was discovered.

We may never know for sure who lived in Machu Picchu. We may always wonder why it was built in a place that was so hard to reach. We may never find out why it was abandoned.

Some day, possibly, we *will* know. Archeologists never stop searching for facts.

But perhaps these questions are better left unanswered. Perhaps it's right that Machu Picchu should forever keep its mysterious — and beautiful — secret.